ELIZABETH TAYLOR BOOK

The Biography of Elizabeth Taylor

University Press

CONTENTS

INTRODUCTION

Standing in the office of a powerful member of the studio, Elizabeth Taylor watched in horror as this man began screaming at her mother. To her 15-year-old eyes, he was not only out of line, but he was doing something for which she would find it nearly impossible to forgive. The man was telling her mother he had pulled her and her daughter out of a gutter, implying that everything they had was owed to him. It was true that her mother had been an actress, but she and her husband had also been successful art dealers while living in England when they had their daughter, Elizabeth Taylor. They had chosen to return to the US to live in LA, but their young daughter was performing even before they made that choice. Taylor had a natural talent for performing, starting with dancing. When she was young, she had put on a recital for Princesses Elizabeth and Margaret – with Princess Elizabeth going on to be the queen of England a couple of decades later. It was clear that whatever this man was saying was inaccurate. Taylor had a problem with how he talked to her loving mother. Elizabeth's talent was why she was there, not some man happy to spout verbal abuse at people around him.

Then she witnessed this powerful figure swear at her mother, and that was the breaking point for the young teenager. She reported later that her response was full of vitriol and emotion, giving the man exactly the same treatment he was giving her mother. She recalled him saying something along the lines of "I took you and your [explitive] daughter out of the gutter." He was talking about her, a 15-year-old teenager who had already been in several movies. He was insulting Elizabeth to her mother while being incredibly verbally aggressive. Outraged, she said she cursed aloud for the first time, telling him that he and his studio could go to hell for how he was treating her mother. She followed that up with the sentiment that she would never return to his office. As she left the office, the young Taylor walked by her mother, who stood with her eyes squeezed shut. Taylor later said that she had the impression that her mother was praying, though what that prayer would have been isn't clear.

Her mother admitted that she was furious, but the situation was also incredibly emotional, so she was in tears. When they talked, she told her that she had to return and apologize to the man she had just witnessed berating her mother. Then someone else from the studio joined the conversation and agreed that she had to return with an apology. Realizing that they were both friends with the horrible man, she was not moved when they talked down to her, according to her memory, saying, "Sweetheart, you have got to go back and apologize." She was not about to listen to their advice, though, and she turned it around, asking them why she should be the one to apologize when he was the one who started it. All she did was stick up for her mother. She told them the same thing she had told the horrid man – she would not return to his office, and she didn't care if they fired her because of it. She later reflected that she had no idea where she found the ability to be so independent, taking a position that was completely her own instead of giving in to what the men were trying to get her to do. The fact that she didn't know how the guy who yelled at her mom would take that kind of backtalk from a young teen did not worry her. Even at that young age, she had a firm understanding of right and wrong that she wasn't willing to compromise. Ultimately, she knew they needed her more than he needed an apology. So she never apologized but remained on the project.

This was one of the defining parts of who she would become in Hollywood. Her talent got Taylor the attention that kept her working through her teenage years; her looks helped to get her parts that were sought by many other actors – as well as a legacy as a heartbreaker; and her sense of right and wrong made her beloved by others in the industry. She would become the highest-paid actor in Hollywood for a time and had many friendships and working relationships with other celebrities (both in Hollywood and outside of it). She lived the kind of life that seemed both charmed and cursed. But to Taylor herself, it was simply life on her own terms.

CHAPTER 1

Early Life

Elizabeth Rosemond Taylor was born into a well-off family and was given the kind of name that would have been a great stage name. Her mother, Sara Taylor, had been a stage actor when she was young, but she had given up acting when she married Francis Taylor. They had their first child, Howard, in 1929, and that same year they moved from the US to London, England, to open an art gallery. They had their second child, Elizabeth, three years after arriving in the country. The children grew up in a fairly privileged environment, which Elizabeth later remembered as being upper-middle class. They had a significantly different upbringing than they would have experienced in the US because of how much more important classes were in the UK. As a result, they were able to socialize with people of much higher stature, including Laura Knight, Augustus

John, and Colonel Victor Cazalet. With parents in the arts, the two children learned a lot about the many different art forms. They spent time with their parents but were raised by their nanny, which was common in the UK. She admitted during one interview that she couldn't stand her nanny but also said that it was probably more because of her desire for independence than anything with the nanny herself. In 1939, life was changing significantly across Europe as World War II began, causing a sense of uncertainty and fear.

Having somewhere else they could go, her parents decided to return to the US instead of staying close to the Germans, who had been wholly underestimated prior to the events leading up to the invasion of France. While most of Europe expected things to be similar to the way they had occurred during World War I, or at least for the technology to be similar, the rest of Europe was shocked by how Germany was able to roll into multiple countries with significantly more advanced weaponry. Many nations were still using cavalry, and the German army had tanks. The speed with which the Germans managed to take over continental Europe was shocking. It was only because of the sacrifice of the French, coupled with the bravery of British sailors (most of whom were not in the military but were individual boat owners or companies with boats), that Great Britain didn't lose a large percentage of their military at Dunkirk.

The Taylors took off for California, and things did not seem to go nearly so well after their return. Their daughter had been an entertainer, dancing in front of royalty in England, but in the US, the social structure was different. They seemed to have financial troubles because Taylor later talked about her father's problems with drinking. She even stated that he was abusive when drunk and would excuse his behavior by saying he didn't know what he was doing. She also said that she could understand why he was upset because she was still young when she started earning more money than he did. He had provided his family with a great lifestyle in England, with the kids having a nanny and horses (Taylor talked about the fact that she had a pony when she was less than five years old). In The US, things seemed to be very different. Her ability to seemingly forgive him for hitting her and taking out his frustration on a child seems admirable, but it is also common for children to forgive parents because they have a bond that is far different than any other kind of bond. Her life did seem to be colored a bit by his anger, so she wasn't quick to excuse him. However, she said that she could understand his reaction better once she had children of her own and was trying to imagine them becoming more of a primary breadwinners as children – she could understand how that was incredibly upsetting to her father. His temper certainly explained why her mother was willing to put up with verbal attacks by men outside the home, even when her daughter was present. Considering the time when she started making movies – the 1940s – which was a time when the world was upside down, with men going off to war and women taking on typical male roles, it was undoubtedly a difficult time for the whole family. The fact that her father didn't go off to war and was also not the breadwinner could have made him try to escape his shame and humiliation by drinking. Without the filters of sobriety, he took out his anger on the person showing him up. What he did certainly was not excusable, but Taylor herself managed to find peace with it and didn't continue to hold it against him over the course of her life.

Her family life contributed to her strong sense of self. Her father was abusive when he was drinking, but he also seemed keen to keep her from being entirely used by Hollywood. Her mother was active in Taylor's career and helped to keep her grounded over the years as she became a teenager. However, it was her brother who seemed to help her the most. She said she worshipped him when they were children because he didn't care about the superficial things that seemed to matter to everyone else. He was non-materialistic and genuine, which must have been incredibly rare for her to find, given how young she was when she started to become famous. They remained close over most of their lives, though they took incredibly different paths. Where she grew up in the spotlight and remained in it for nearly all of her life, he cultivated his own privacy. She said that she always made sure that she didn't "inflict my fame on him" because she didn't want him to have to deal with the same problems she did. He loved his privacy and had no interest in the kind of lifestyle that fame offered.

For all of the family's flaws, Taylor reported that she always felt they were her support group. There was a myth, likely pushed by higher-ups in Hollywood, that the studios were like one big family and that they worked to cultivate and nurture talent. Taylor laughed at the idea, saying that it was clear from the beginning that they were just using her, even though she was just a child. Although studio heads tried to portray themselves positively, like a family, she replied that it was much more like a factory. It was her family who gave her the love and support that she needed to do well. Considering how openly rebellious she was, refusing to accept horrible treatment for her or her mother, it is clear that it wasn't the studio or Hollywood helping her learn and grow. Instead, they were teaching her to stand up and refuse to be treated that way. Much of that support she attributed to her family.

CHAPTER 2

Child Actor

Taylor had performed for an audience before they reached LA, so the transfer into movies wasn't exactly unexpected. Since her father was in the art industry, he had a number of contacts in Hollywood, opening the door for her to move into the industry. Initially, her mother was not entirely sold on the idea. She had acted on stage, so she had an idea of just how rough things could be. The idea of her young daughter joining that world was not entirely palatable to the more protective former actress. After meeting the chairman at Universal Picture studio, she finally relented, allowing her daughter to go in for a screen test. With Taylor's outgoing personality and disarming friendliness, especially for someone so young, she was soon cast in her first movie. She began filming in 1942, and soon her first movie, There's One Born Every Minute, was released in theaters. Though they had been impressed by her at first, Universal Pictures soon dropped the nine-year-old actor, which could have ended her career if she hadn't already gotten the attention of MGM Studios.

The new studio was intrigued by the young actor, so they offered her a contract, a feat that would have been considered a great deal today. However, in the early 20th century, contracts tended to be particularly horrible, especially for women. The contracts often specified how much an actor could weigh and not be in breach of contract, frequently creating problems for women both on and off the screen. Protections were almost absent, while studios controlled as many aspects of a woman's life as possible. Men were also controlled to some extent but were far less rigorously monitored, with many of the notable actors from the time not particularly good-looking. This is perhaps why Taylor laughed at the idea that studios were similar to families – they didn't foster so much as control their actors. In most instances, if an actor didn't do what the studio wanted, the actor would soon be unemployed, and they would find it nearly impossible to find work again.

However, Taylor seemed to be an exception, even when she was a child. Her strong will and sense of right and wrong did not appear to be deal breakers because she was so captivating on screen. Her next movie was *Lassie Come Home*, which was released in 1943. MGM's belief in her abilities paid off the next year with the release of *National Velvet*. This was likely a movie that played toward the young actor's strengths because it was about a young girl who saved a horse. Having grown up owning a pony when she was young, Taylor had no problem working with the horse on the set, even finding it to be very comforting. The girl in the movie soon trained her horse to race, giving Taylor an interest in more thrilling endeavors.

With two of her earliest movies having her work with animals, it played into the positive experiences she had with animals in her personal life. Over the rest of her life, Taylor was known for being a great lover of animals, even living in Africa with one of her husbands, where she went on to have some unique interactions with wild animals. She survived some of these experiences and understood the wild animals because she worked with animals in situations that were entirely unnatural earlier in her life. It could have given her a much better understanding of reading the body language of animals. Even with experts telling her how to deal with an encounter with a lion, Taylor ignored the "expert advice," managing to come out of the experience with no problems.

Beyond the studios and her father's abuse, Taylor had her own problems that began to mar her young life. Her first serious medical condition began to manifest during this time. She learned how to work with chronic back pain because of scoliosis. This was further exacerbated when she was 12 years old and fell off a horse. Some of her later problems with substance abuse could be tied to the pain she experienced at a young age.

CHAPTER 3

Marrying Young

Taylor had established herself as a child actor, but she was only just out of childhood when she first married. At just 18 years old, she married for the first time in 1950, a time when it was still fairly common for women to marry while they were very young. As someone incredibly passionate, this made a lot of sense for the headstrong actor. Her first husband was Conrad Hilton, who was better known as Nicky. He was 23 when they wed, and he was a hotel heir of the Hilton family, catching her attention perhaps because of a lifestyle that seemed similar to hers. One of her first roles as an adult had just finished wrapping when they married, and it was appropriately themed – Father of the Bride. Since she married around the same time the movie was released, the studio paid for her dress and some of the wedding celebrations. As a result, a good bit of the day was filmed for promotional use for the movie. The couple had more than 600 people invited to the ceremony. And outside of where they said their vows were several thousand fans hoping to get a glimpse of the famous actress and her stylish new husband. Though she had seen what marriage could be like with her parents, she wed while still "very naïve" of what marriage was actually like.

They wed on May 6, 1950, but it was easily one of her worst and shortest marriages. Perhaps because he was raised as an heir, Nicky felt entitled to certain things, which in retrospect made no sense as he married a well-known actress. He was incredibly jealous and angry from the very beginning of their marriage. She had related her experience of her first marriage as being on the rocks before they had finished their honeymoon. They went to Europe for 14 weeks, and during that time, he let her see who he actually was. The famous actor wrote several short books about her life (though she said none of them was a real autobiography). She wrote about her first husband in the one she published in 1988, saying that while they were still on their honeymoon, he "became sullen, angry, and abusive, physically and mentally." As she had already proven with the studio just a few years earlier, she was unwilling to sit by and allow herself to be abused. Less than a year after they married – and before she was 19 years old, she was already going through her first divorce. It was finalized on January 29, 1951.

This experience at such a young age could be why she was far less willing to continue in a marriage when she wasn't happy, despite divorce being taboo for most of her life. She only had two marriages that lasted longer than five years, most of which ended before divorce became more acceptable.

She waited for a little over a year before marrying again, this time to someone much older than her. Working with Michael Wilding on the set of *Ivanhoe*, she was drawn to the much older man (20 years older) who had the kind of calm demeanor and even temperament that her first husband entirely lacked. It has been widely reported that he was a very positive influence on her because she had someone who supported her and kept things calmer, at least in the early days. They had two sons together, the first in 1953 and the second in 1955. Unfortunately, jealousy again became a problem for a different reason this time. As an established actor a couple of decades older than his young bride, Wilding seemed upset that she was increasingly getting more work and gaining more attention while his star seemed to be waning. The initially calming presence did not last, and after five years of marriage, they finally agreed to a divorce in 1957. How he acted, or at least the reasons for his behavior, reminded her of her experience with her father. She was again doing increasingly better than her husband, which would have been hard for a man to stomach in the 1950s. Instead of supporting her and providing the same comfortable and safe place, her husband's jealousy that his wife was accomplishing more contributed to the marriage breaking down.

If Taylor had been able to find a husband who wasn't nearly so possessive or offended by her star power, perhaps she would have settled down and been known for a long-lasting relationship. But unfortunately, the only people who had insight into her rising star were people who had their own problems.

While her luck with marriage was abysmal, her performances during this time were spell-binding, perhaps because of some of the people she worked with in what is now considered to be part of the Golden Age of film. In *Father of the Bride*, she played a woman who insisted on marrying her boyfriend, who was less than acceptable to her middle-class father, a character played by Spencer Tracy. By the time her first marriage failed, she was already working on her next great movie, *A Place in the Sun*. This role showcased a much different character for the actress. She was in a love triangle that ended badly for two of the three characters. She was the daughter of a wealthy man, and her character fell in love with a poor man working for his rich uncle. The male love interest was George Eastman, who had been having an affair with one of the factory women at his uncle's business. When he tries to leave her for Taylor's character, the young factory worker drowns. He is found guilty of murder. It was a much different kind of movie for Taylor, and it introduced her to one of her best-known friends, Montgomery Clift.

As her second marriage was in its last year, she starred in another career-defining role with several other important actors in *Giant*. She met another lifelong friend there, Rock Hudson, and they played a married couple. However, the movie is best remembered for being the last role of James Dean before he died.

Now well into adulthood and with much more life experience, her roles became increasingly more complicated as her personal life started to take a dark turn.

CHAPTER 4

Off-Screen

Early in her life, Taylor did not seem happy being alone because there was very little time between marriages. Perhaps inspired by how comfortable her first marriage was to an older man, she chose a partner who was even older as her next paramour. Mike Tod was a producer and 25 years older than the young actor. He had found his success, even earning an Oscar as a producer on Around the World in 80 Days. Their marriage happened remarkably quickly because she was pregnant with his child about a month after her second divorce was finalized. This was her first daughter. Over their marriage, he was more than happy to give her gifts and express his affection through jewelry. Given how famous her eyes had become at the time – she is still known for her violet-colored eyes – many of her husbands during this period would give her lots of jewelry, which would become another defining part of her public persona. The way they show on her neck or dangling from her ears was rarely as bright as her famous eyes.

Later in her life, Taylor would say that he was her first real love, even claiming she was "happiest with Mike Todd." How much of that is based on their short time together is uncertain, but it was the one marriage that did not end in divorce. The couple married in February 1957. A little over a year later, in March 1958, the couple was supposed to take a trip on his plane, but Taylor had fallen ill. Opting to stay home and recover, she wasn't on the plane when it crashed, killing her husband. With three children and suddenly a widower, Taylor's life was thrown into a type of chaos where she was trying to grieve and raise three young children. She also wasn't particularly comfortable being alone. This may have contributed to seeing her public personality shift significantly over the next few years.

Around this time, she appeared in one of her most well-known and celebrated roles as Maggie Pollitt, wife of Brick Pollitt, a football star who no longer plays. Her husband was played by the illustrious Paul Newman, known for being one of the most faithful men in Hollywood. Newman was married to his first wife when he met Joanne Woodward. Newman and Woodward fought their attraction for several years, but after starring in a movie together, they felt it was impossible to keep fighting, and his wife seemed to agree, granting him a divorce. He married Woodward around the time *Cat on a Hot Tin Roof* was released. In the years after this, he expressed how he had no interest in anyone else, even stunning women like Taylor, because he loved Woodward too much. They were married for 50 years until he died in 2008. This is an interesting juxtaposition considering Taylor was experiencing her own crisis at the time, though not of her choice. The two do work very well together on screen, and the fact that they are a married couple experiencing difficulties could have been reflective of where they were in their personal lives. The movie earned six Academy Award nominations but didn't win any categories. Taylor would later say that she was glad she pressed on and did the movie after her husband died because it helped her to feel something other than sorrow. Initially, she had felt that she didn't care if she died following her husband's death, which would likely contribute to what came next in her life.

Taylor had become friends with many of the people who had been friends with her late husband, including Eddie Fisher, who was married to the famous actor Debbie Reynolds. What came next made tabloid headlines and earned Taylor the reputation as a homewrecker. She and Fisher got close as they grieved the death of Todd. Taylor would later say that Fisher's marriage was already in trouble, and she said that it bothered her how the media would depict her after she and Fisher started an affair, resulting in the end of his marriage. Even if his marriage was in trouble, Taylor certainly played a significant role in ensuring it ended. However, Fisher should have received much more negative publicity than he did. He was the one who was married and made a choice to cheat on his wife. However, tabloids and the media were far harsher toward Taylor, possibly because she was more famous, and it was more entertaining to read about her as more of a villain, a role that she hadn't played in films. Fisher was a famous singer, but Taylor was a glamorous actor who had been married three times, while Fisher was married to his first wife (he would go on to marry four more times after his first wife). What seemed to make Taylor look even more like a villain was that she was friends with Reynolds. The media did seem to be harsher toward Taylor, but there were significant career repercussions for Fisher, who had his television show canceled because of the scandal.

Taylor and Reynolds would eventually end up having dinner sometime during the 1960s or 1970s while aboard *Queen Elizabeth*. Reynolds had reached out first, resulting in Taylor inviting her to dinner. They ended up on friendly terms after that, with Reynolds even saying she ended up better off with the divorce. She also told Oprah Winfrey years later that she had no chance against Taylor, who was long considered one of the most attractive women in the world. She even compared what happened between her, her ex, and Taylor to Jennifer Aniston, Brad Pitt, and Angelina Jolie, which played out in a similar way (though Pitt did take a lot more flak in the media than Fisher). She would admit that she was lucky to work with a wide range of legendary men in Hollywood, including Clark Gabel, and Fred Astaire (who helped her during a particularly difficult time on *Singing in the Rain*), without ever being romantically connected to any of them. She said she was essentially a novice compared to the voluptuous and experienced Taylor. After a few years, she even learned how to parent with her ex because it was important to her two children, Todd and Carrie Fisher (who would later become a Hollywood legend in her own right). Reynolds and Taylor even seemed to be friends again when Taylor died, having spoken just a couple of weeks before her death.

Part of what helped Reynolds later was the fact that she felt that Taylor never actually loved Fisher. As Taylor had once said, Fisher and Reynolds weren't in a happy marriage, so what was she (Taylor) supposed to do, sleep alone? Reynolds firmly believed that Fisher was more of a placeholder until Taylor found someone better suited to her life. Since her marriage with Fisher started with so much turmoil, the couple was not nearly as welcomed elsewhere, which did not bother Taylor so much. Unfortunately, Fisher's career never recovered, and his second marriage failed after five years.

CHAPTER 5

Richard Burton

Once their marriage became official – on the same day that Fisher's divorce was finalized with Reynolds – the media didn't cover the couple except to vilify Taylor. She starred in Suddenly, Last Summer, the same year she and Fisher married. She starred with her friend Montgomery Clift and the legendary Katharine Hepburn again.

While her husband's career suffered, Taylor seemed to be in even more demand, perhaps because she could lean into how she was portrayed. Her next major role was as Cleopatra, a woman who, to this day, is still considered more of a femme fatale, making it a nearly perfect role for the woman who was portrayed similarly in the 1960s. The studio offered her a million-dollar contract to portray the famous – or to some notorious – Queen of Ancient

Egypt, making her the first woman to be signed for that amount. When asked about it, she replied, "If someone is dumb enough to offer me a million dollars to make a picture, I'm certainly not dumb enough to turn it down." By this time, she was incredibly business savvy, which is why she was the highest-paid female actor in the world for a while. In addition to high paychecks, she required that studios give her gifts to be in their movies, something she could do because of how reliable she was as a draw in the cinema. The studio was taking a huge risk by offering her so much, considering her reputation at the time. They made the offer in 1963, and many people were still angry about her scandal from nearly five years earlier. The movie itself was wildly over budget, and the filming was problematic. The film was originally going o be filmed in England, but they moved to Rome because the weather in the UK was causing Taylor health problems. They rewrote the entire script, recasting many roles. The movie had an enormous budget, yet it still managed to go over. It was an amazing set that was visually remarkable but not without many problems. Also, the move to Rome proved to be just as problematic, and Taylor got sick. The set was cold because of the freezing rain. Because she was sick, she had to use a drip hidden from the camera at one point. She refused to keep shooting until they installed heating. Many cast members praised the way the legendary actress treated them, and they were thankful for the warmth while wearing skimpier outfits.

The fierce passion between Taylor and one of her co-stars, Richard Burton, stood out the most. The seasoned actor once again found herself in the spotlight for all of the wrong reasons. People wanted to dislike her, and the fact that she was not able to keep her passion in check around the married Burton gave people confirmation of the earlier accusations – she was a homewrecker. Again, Taylor wasn't alone in starting the affair, and Burton was equally passionate as Taylor. He was just as much at fault as Taylor, and he was just as big a star as her. They had met about a decade before they worked on the film, but once they were reunited, neither of them could keep themselves in check. Taylor would tell an interviewer, "When I saw him on the set of *Cleopatra*, I fell in love and I have loved him ever since, practically my whole adult life."

Both were incredibly passionate, and with tabloids all over the set, it became clear that they were having an affair. They both divorced their respective spouses and married in March of 1964. Burton became Taylor's fifth husband, but she was only his second wife. His first marriage lasted from 1949 to 1963, and he divorced his wife to marry Taylor. He adopted her daughter with Todd, and when Taylor's adoption of another daughter went through after they married, he also adopted the second daughter.

The couple would act together several times

throughout their marriage, with one of the most memorable being *Who's Afraid of Virginia Woolf?* In 1966. The couple acted in the movie together, playing an older married couple (middle-aged) who have invited a younger couple over to dinner. Burton was a professor, and the husband of the couple they invited to dinner was a new member of the faculty, so they were coworkers. The older couple spends the evening trading verbal barbs, stunning the young couple. It is very likely that people watching felt they were getting insight into the relationship between Taylor and Burton, at least in retrospect. That does seem unlikely, though, as they were passionate, not a couple who seemed to be openly hostile and without love. The problem is that they likely didn't have to fully act for the movie because they did fight often, and not always in private.

The couple continued to prove lucrative for the tabloids because they had a notoriously tumultuous relationship, with some saying that they had too much passion and emotions involved. Fighting was incredibly common; eventually, the fights made it difficult for the couple to remain together. They ended up working together on a movie called *Divorce His, Divorce Hers*. Following the movie's end, they went through their own divorce in 1974.

However, the pair were not yet done with each other, and it seemed like they were no sooner divorced than they were against making their vows to each other. This time they went to Botswana and married in a small ceremony in 1975. They had a home in Africa, and Taylor found it to be a great place to escape all of the drama that followed her with the media. In 1988, she took part in a more in-depth interview with *Rolling Stone*, talking about how she eventually gained the trust of monkeys in the area. Eventually, she got them to come into her living room, and she would enjoy their company and relax. Perhaps because of how many good times and memories she and Burton had in Africa, they hoped to recapture those times. Unfortunately, they weren't able to find whatever they sought. Their first marriage was Taylor's longest, lasting about a decade. The second marriage to Burton didn't last a year before they once again called it quits, this time for good. She would later say when asked about him, "Even when we could no longer live together, we continued to love each other. To this day, my feelings for him are so strong I cannot speak about him without being overcome with emotion."

With the end of her romantic relationship with Burton, Taylor seems to take an entirely different direction in her life.

CHAPTER 6

Semi-Retirement

One thing that is fairly clear looking at Taylor's career is that by the time she was in her 40s, she had fewer people looking to cast her in roles. By the time her relationship with Burton was over, she was in her mid-40s, and her reputation made it harder for her to find the kind of companionship she wanted. There were rumors that she was spending more time in Washington, DC, at this time because she had taken an interest in one of the ambassadors in the town. If that rumor were true, it would have been far more shocking than her next relationship. It made sense to spend time in DC since, in LA, she was getting less work. Her roles became smaller, partly because she no longer looked like she did when she was in her teens to her 30s. She gained weight, and while the studios no longer could control an actor's weight, they didn't have to seek out people they felt didn't meet a certain visual aesthetic. The younger people were drawn to younger actors, while older people were still upset by the reputation she developed after so many failed marriages and high-profile scandals. She simply wasn't the draw she used to be, so she didn't get the kind of attention she did from 1940 to the 1960s. By the time she divorced Burton for the second time.

By this stage in her life, Taylor didn't seem so interested in acting, though that may have much to do with her next husband. Once again, she only stayed single long after divorcing Burton. Her next husband was John Warner, a Virginian politician. This meant that Taylor didn't disappear from the spotlight, but she transitioned to a completely different kind of lifestyle. Warner was a Republican in an area after the scandal that saw President Nixon having to leave office because of his own scandals. Given how outspoken Taylor was, it is a very poor fit for people today. The Republican Party was a very different party in the 1970s, with many popular actors and celebrities aligning with them. Taylor met Warner when he was asked to escort her to an event in Washington, DC. Queen Elizabeth was the host of the dinner, so it was being held at the British Embassy. It seemed that both of them felt something when they met, though, given her track record, it was likely that Taylor felt compelled to find another partner. Since she was 18 years old, she hadn't been single between her marriages for a full year. Her relationship started not too long after her previous divorce was completed. Notably, she would make it clear that what she was looking for by this time was more about companionship than passion and romance.

At the time, he was asked to be her escort because he was the head of the American Revolution Bicentennial Administration, and she was a high-profile figure. It ended up feeling more like a blind date, and they admitted to being a bit awkward. Unlike what she was accustomed to, Warner was driving his own car – he didn't arrive to pick her up with a chauffeur. This took her by surprise, and Taylor asked him if he was used to driving himself, to which he was likely confused, as he responded yes. It was only when they were finally headed back to her place that they finally found a topic they could enjoy – Warner mentioned that he had a horse farm. Ever the consummate animal lover, Taylor quickly jumped into the topic, and the conversation finally flowed. Not long after that evening, they attended events together. They married at the end of that year, with this wedding occurring on the future senator's farm. Since she was well-known for her love of jewelry by this point, Warner got her a ring that would reflect his own passions, resulting in her getting a red, white, and blue jewel-encrusted ring.

They seemed to live quite happily on the farm, but soon, Taylor realized just how restrictive it was to be a politician's spouse. She was his second wife, and life on the farm was very different from the public life she experienced with him. From early in their marriage, he talked about how his wife was happily living on the farm, helping to take care of the tasks that go with farm life, such as branding a calf. He also talked about how they planned to cure their own hams. How happy she was with these activities is not quite clear because she did love animals, but he seemed to focus on things that harmed or killed animals. It seemed that he was making it sound like the seductress had finally settled down with him, living the kind of life of "the stereotypical American" instead of the person she was with her previous husbands. For whatever he said, though, he did seem aware that her interest in the farm was a large part of why she took such an interest in him, once quipping, "I think she fell in love with the farm, and I guess I came along with the horses." How the relationship may have continued had they stuck to the more mundane life is unsure because Warner would soon decide to run to be one of Virginia's Senators.

Initially, Taylor didn't seem too adverse to the idea of his political aspirations. When he went to campaign, she joined him, and the large crowds that the couple drew weren't there because they were interested in hearing what he had to say as a candidate. This could have been problematic, as it had been in her previous relationships with men. The difference was that it got him the attention that politicians need to get their name out there. Unfortunately, the experience was not positive for Taylor, who had several health issues by this point. When they were in Richmond, she ended up in the hospital because a little metal managed to get under her eyelid. They went to Norfolk, where she hurt her back when one of her heels got caught on a carpet. This caused the couple to be late to the event he was supposed to attend. One of the next places they went, she wound up back n a hospital because a chicken bone got caught in her throat. As if this weren't bad enough for her, John Belushi relentlessly mocked the injury on *Saturday Night Live*.

He managed to win his race, but her health problems continued after the election ended. Now Warner had to choose between work and his wife as she spent time in the hospital, and he did what you would expect of a politician. He visited her when he could, but she was largely left alone. As her husband spent more time in DC and being a Senator, she drank more and tried to find a way to occupy herself on a large farm. She had to watch what she wore, with people instructing her that she could wear purple – a color she often wore because it was associated with royalty. By her wearing the color, it associated her husband with the antiquated idea of a color representing royalty in the modern day. Between her health issues and loneliness, she gained weight to the point that she was no longer considered someone Hollywood could really include.

Seeking another path forward, she decided to go to New York City, where she got a role in a Broadway play, showing that stage performances were far less particular about looks and far more interested in talent. Just like when she was in the hospital, her husband would come to visit her when he could. She started working in New York in 1981, and by 1982, both knew that their marriage had reached a place where it made sense to end it.

Taylor was straightforward about what they were to each other from the start. She talked about their relationship not long after it ended, saying, "He knows he wasn't the love of my life. And I know I wasn't the love of his life. But we loved each other. We got along wonderfully until he decided to be a politician. And then he married the Senate." This hints at some bitterness on her part, which would be understandable. Being married to her and having her support boosted his profile, drawing the kinds of crowds that most politicians dream of having early in their career. However, when he took on a more dedicated political role, he ceased to be what she needed because he wasn't available to her in the way she needed.

They did remain friends, and he would occasionally join her as her escort to different events, but they no longer had any of the illusion that they were anything more than friends. Taylor would be single for a long stretch for the first time in her life. And it seemed problematic for her as she has so many issues with which to contend, both in her personal and professional life.

CHAPTER 7

Later Years

T hough she cared about Warner, it seemed like Taylor was never particularly happy in the marriage. One time when she was at Studio 54, she was spending time with Liza Minnelli and Betty Ford. She was reported abusing substances, including alcohol and prescription medications. After a few years of loneliness, the marriage ended, and Taylor was left to face several issues she had after years of difficult relationships with men, work, and the media. Before she ended up back in another relationship that didn't meet her needs, several of her children, friends, and perhaps most importantly, her brother made sure she stopped and faced herself. There was a lot for her to do, starting with taking care of herself.

For the first time since she was 18 years old, Taylor stayed single as she began to take care of herself.

Instead of marrying again, she entered rehab at the Betty Ford Center and spent several years as a single woman. As a result, she would begin to think about her life and her own experiences differently. Getting treated for her dependencies, she finally had the chance to consider what she wanted and the direction she wanted to take her life.

From 1976 to 1982, she was largely out of the public eye as she took a break from her career. She focused on herself for a while. Deciding to go in for treatment at a center would have been incredibly difficult because there was a significant stigma around mental health and addiction in the 1980s. People would again make fun of celebrities who sought help for addiction (something that is still, unfortunately, a problem; they are seeking treatment for a problem, so making jokes about it makes other people less likely to want to seek help). When she decided to go in for treatment in 1983, the center had only been open for about a year, and she was the first big-name celebrity to go there. Her decision to seek help would make it more normalized for celebrities. The Better Ford Center would become an incredibly popular place when celebrities finally acknowledged when they needed help.

She ended up back at the center in 1988, finding that she still needed help. During this second time, she met Larry Fortensky, a construction worker who was also there as a patient. During that time at the center, people, including movie stars, were expected to live a very basic life. She was expected to clean floors and make her bed in the morning, something that she had not done much throughout her life. It was a stark contrast to Fortensky, who hadn't finished high school, had grown up in a small town, and had already had two failed marriages. He was a lot of things that she wasn't accustomed to, and she seemed incredibly taken with the idea of something so refreshingly different. This always seemed to be a significant draw for her. He would say that she approached him, and though he knew who she was, he had not seen any of her movies. She took to calling him by one of two nicknames, Stallion, and Larry the Lion, probably because of his thick, long blonde hair. Though she was connected with a lot of men after rehab, she and Larry married in October 1991. This has been the longest stint of Taylor being single in her adult life up to that point. She was far more calculating and cautious about who she chose. She chose someone more likely to consider her needs instead of looking for ways to use her or compete with her. He had not given her an engagement ring, making him probably the only man who didn't try to woo her with jewelry, and it did not seem to bother Taylor.

The wedding was held at Neverland, the home of Michael Jackson, who was a friend of Taylor. Their wedding was a spectacle, and the media was in a frenzy over it. Security even had to throw out a media member who tried to parachute into the event. The best pictures from the wedding were taken by someone paid by Taylor. The seasoned actress was well aware of how much the media would make of her eighth marriage, so she sold the images taken to *People Magazine*, once again for the hefty sum of $1 million. In 1988, that was a huge sum of money, but she had a plan for those funds.

Once married to the legendary actress, Fortensky continued to work, as he would explain later, "I am a proud man and I like to work. I didn't want her money. I'd get up at 6 am to go to the construction site. Elizabeth would get up, put on a kaftan, and we'd have breakfast. She'd go back to bed after I left." He said he loved how she could be incredibly innocent with him. It certainly wasn't the image that most people had of her, so he pulled out what he said was his favorite picture of her, with her in a nightdress on and a fur coat flailing her arms in the snow. When he reflected on the story, it was clear how much he adored the time he had with her, saying, "We were in bed and she sat up and said, 'I want to make a snow angel.' She grabbed a fur coat and put it over her nightdress. I chased her outside and she fell in the snow and started waving her arms around giggling like a little girl." He would say that despite being a couple decades older than him, she never seemed old to him.

Perhaps she began to feel the same loneliness with him that she felt with her previous husbands, so she began to pressure him to quit working so they could travel.

Like her other marriages, though, neither of them were happy for very long. Her health continued to be a problem, causing him to sleep in a different room from her because of several surgeries she underwent. However, the fact that the media would not leave them alone really got to Fortensky. He was never comfortable with the fact that there were almost always cameras around them, no matter where they went, and it ultimately made him unhappy. After five years, Taylor knew that the marriage was over, so she told him that she wasn't happy anymore, and she was aware that he wasn't either. However, she still cared about him and said that she didn't want them to end up hating each other. The divorce was finalized on October 31, 1996. He resumed the life had had before marrying her, and Taylor went on to be single for the rest of her life. They did remain friends, and they spoke not long before her death.

Though the media was quick to sensationalize most parts of her life, they didn't talk much about her health, which had been an issue since she was a child. Born with scoliosis, some of the stunts on set caused her additional pain. When working on the film *Elephant Walk*, Taylor was nearly blinded by a rusty splinter and had to go in for emergency surgery. She contracted pneumonia while working on *Butterfield 9*. She was pronounced dead four times, even having to get a tracheotomy to save her life. She would have another near-fatal bout with the illness in 1990. The media heavily discussed her addiction in the 1980s, and she was treated poorly for trying to get better. She had both hips replaced in 1994. Following a stroke in 1997, she underwent brain surgery to remove a benign tumor. A few years later, she was treated for skin cancer. She underwent spinal surgery in 2004 and seemed almost amused when people were shocked that she was still alive, pointing to how resilient she had been over the years. In 2004, she was diagnosed with what would finally cause her death, congestive heart failure. Despite the diagnosis, she did manage to live another seven years. She was hospitalized in January 2011 because of her condition, then died on March 23, 2011.

CHAPTER 8

A Legacy

W hat the media tended to ignore for the more sensational and scandalous headlines was the woman behind the glamor. Taylor was an incredibly loyal and loving friend, treating people with the understanding many fail to have. Two of her close friends, Montgomery Clift and Rock Hudson, were gay when it was unacceptable, but Taylor didn't care. She remained good friends with them, though it might have been refreshing for her to have men who only wanted friendship from her as she was considered a sex symbol. When she was nearing the end of her marriage to her second husband, they had managed to throw a party at their home in Beverly Hills. She had invited Clift because they were incredibly close. At first, he didn't want to go because he knew that the marriage was failing, and he felt awkward being around them when they were together. He went, and the party was largely a disaster. When he left, he got into a nearly fatal car accident when trying to navigate a corkscrew road in extremely foggy conditions. One of their other mutual friends had been in front of Clift when the accident occurred, and he immediately returned to Taylor's house to get help. She demanded to be taken to her friend. Upon reaching the scene, she disregarded her safety, quickly getting into the destroyed car where her friends were seriously injured, going through the back window because of how damaged the rest was. Seeing that her friend wasn't moving, she crawled into him and began trying to do whatever she could to keep him alive. He was disfigured, and the impact had knocked some of his teeth in his throat. After calling out to him and realizing that he was choking on something, Taylor opened his mouth and removed the teeth blocking his air passage. Had she not acted, he would have died because it took an hour for the ambulance to reach them. Cameras were there by that point, and she ensured they couldn't get a picture of Clift as he was put on a stretcher and taken to the hospital. To ensure that no one sensationalized the situation, she warned the paparazzi that if any of them took a single image of him, she would never allow them to take a picture of her again. This worked, and no pictures of him were published following the accident. Clift would receive reconstructive surgery, but he would never look quite like he had before the accident. She would have nightmares from the accident and then watch her good friend start abusing substances, as his career was not what he wanted after the accident. His last film was The Misfits, which was also Marilyn Monroe's last role. She also had a very troubled time in Hollywood, and she would see someone in as much pain as herself in Clift. When talking about the 1961 film, she would say of one of her co-stars that Clift was "the only person I know who is in worse shape than I am." He died in 1966 at just 45 years old.

Taylor and Hudson also remained good friends, but he suffered a different kind of painful end. He contracted HIV/AIDS, which was kept secret from the media because of the stigma around the disease in the 1980s – it wasn't even talked about or acknowledged by many politicians and celebrities. It was also seen as a righteous disease that killed gay people for their sins, showing how misinformation put many more people at risk and why the disease should have been more openly discussed. Taylor knew her friend was dying, so she managed to sneak into his hospital room to say goodbye just before he died in 1985.

When she married Fortensky in 1988 and sold the pictures to the media, she used the money to help start the Elizabeth Taylor AIDS Foundation, which was finally established in 1991. Her work to ensure that more was done to understand and fight the disease made the disease something people started discussing in the 1990s. Awareness about the disease was spread in large part because of what she did.

Taylor often stood up for celebrities who had been ostracized or were treated poorly by the media because she understood what they were going through. She was also well aware that many times, the media misrepresented events. She protected her friends who were gay and ended up making friends with many people in the gay community before it was acceptable. She befriended Elton John, even after he started being open about his sexuality and several other notable LGBTQ communities. Perhaps more controversially, she even sided with Michael Jackson when he was being investigated for child molestation. She didn't believe the charges and felt he was being vilified by the media, who didn't understand him. During one interview, she said they had a lot in common, and Taylor and Jackson became good friends. She talked about being in bed with him and one of his younger relatives, watching TV and giggling. Pointing out that she had started working and being used for studio money when she was just nine years old, she said he was only three years old when he started being exploited. Given that they both started working while they were still children, it is possible that they spent much of their lives trying to have a childhood. Their experiences certainly meant that they did not have the same outlook on the world because people had been telling them what to do, act, and look for decades.

Jackson was found not guilty of the charges, though the rumors about him continued to swirl for years, even after his death. She stuck by his side and defended him long after the media lost most of their interest in his case.

Taylor managed to have a much longer acting career than many women, largely because of how outspoken she was. From a young age, she refused to change her signature black hair (a really good move as it framed her eyes much better than blond), and she wouldn't allow the studios to change her name. As she aged, she learned not to care about her weight, even though it meant that she largely retired because of it. She earned recognition for her work, with decades of working with many of the biggest names in the Golden Age of Hollywood. She won numerous awards, including two Oscars. One of her sons would recall growing up with the famous actor and having trophies around the house that she would allow them to play with, except for her Oscars. Her children were not allowed to play with those. She was given the title of Dame Elizabeth Taylor, earning the title because she was born in the UK and was considered British. She had tried to renounce her US citizenship when she married Burton, though the story behind why she did that is unclear. When she married Warner, she reacquired her US citizenship. She was a dual citizen of the US and the UK when she died.

CONCLUSION

There was more to the woman than the media portrayed, and she had a rich life outside her marriages and public persona. She lived a fuller life than most people can manage, and she didn't live in a constant state of regret for things that didn't work. At a time when women were treated very differently from men, she refused to back down or give in when she didn't agree. She was valuable enough to the studios that they gave in to her demands more often than not. What surprises most people is that she never received professional acting training, saying that she worked with people with such extensive training and abilities that she learned from them instead of seeking professional training. Working with big names like Paul Newman, Marlon Brando, James Dean, Montgomery Clift, and Laurence Olivier, it is easy to see why she would feel that way – those actors are well-known for the different acting schools.

Taylor was unique in an industry that wanted carbon copies to be more predictable. With many highs and lows over her life, she remains an intriguing figure a decade after her death.

Made in the USA
Thornton, CO
04/21/23 09:31:04

53825cd0-4cc5-4c83-927c-e73c881ede69R01